FREDERICK DOUGLASS'S FOURTH OF JULY SPEECH

FRONT SEAT OF HISTORY: FAMOUS SPEECHES

TAMRA ORR

CHERRY LAKE PRESS

Published in the United States of America by Cherry Lake Publishing Group
Ann Arbor, Michigan
www.cherrylakepublishing.com

Reading Adviser: Marla Conn, MS, Ed., Literacy specialist, Read-Ability, Inc.
Content Adviser: Adam Fulton Johnson, PhD, Assistant Professor, History, Philosophy, and Sociology of Science, Michigan State University
Photo credits: © Glasshouse Images/Alamy Stock Photo, cover; © Everett Historical/Shutterstock.com, 5, 20, 25, 28 [bottom], 29; © Sean Pavone/Shutterstock.com, 6; © National Park Service, FRDO 246, 8; © National Park Service, FRDO 3912, 9; © Library of Congress, LC-DIG-ppmsca-54232, 10; © Zodar/Shutterstock.com, 13; © Library of Congress, LC-DIG-highsm-09902, 14; © MARKA/Alamy Stock Photo, 16; © Matt Gibson/Shutterstock.com, 19; © Brendan Howard/Shutterstock.com, 23; © National Park Service, 24; © Library of Congress, LC-DIG-ppmsca-03128, 26; © Library of Congress, LC-USZ62-93268, 28 [top]

Cherry Lake Press is an imprint of Cherry Lake Publishing Group.

Library of Congress Cataloging-in-Publication Data
Names: Orr, Tamra, author.
Title: Frederick Douglass's Fourth of July speech / Tamra Orr.
Description: Ann Arbor, Michigan : Cherry Lake Publishing, 2021 | Series: Front seat of history: famous speeches | Includes index. | Audience: Grades 4-6
Identifiers: LCCN 2020005660 (print) | LCCN 2020005661 (ebook) | ISBN 9781534168770 (hardcover) | ISBN 9781534170452 (paperback) | ISBN 9781534172296 (pdf) | ISBN 9781534174139 (ebook)
Subjects: LCSH: Slavery—United States—Juvenile literature. | Antislavery movements—United States—Juvenile literature. | Slavery and the church—United States—Juvenile literature. | Fourth of July—Juvenile literature. | Fourth of July orations—Juvenile literature.
Classification: LCC E449 .O77 2021 (print) | LCC E449 (ebook) | DDC 306.3/620973—dc23
LC record available at https://lccn.loc.gov/2020005660
LC ebook record available at https://lccn.loc.gov/2020005661

Cherry Lake Publishing Group would like to acknowledge the work of the Partnership for 21st Century Learning, a Network of Battelle for Kids. Please visit http://www.battelleforkids.org/networks/p21 for more information.

Printed in the United States of America
Corporate Graphics

ABOUT THE AUTHOR

Tamra Orr is the author of more than 500 nonfiction books for readers of all ages. A graduate of Ball State University, she now lives in the Pacific Northwest with her family. When she isn't writing books, she is either camping, reading or on the computer researching the latest topics.

TABLE OF CONTENTS

CHAPTER 1

The Fifth of July

In the 1850s, the United States was truly a nation divided. **Abolitionists** *were against slavery, while Southern states supported it. The Fugitive Slave Act passed in 1850 and was a win for slaveholders. It required that runaway slaves be returned to their owners, even if the slaves were now living in a free state. However, around the same time came the publication of Harriet Beecher Stowe's novel* Uncle Tom's Cabin, *which fueled anti-slavery support. It told, in painful detail, what life as a slave was like. The book was becoming a national best seller. Throughout the country, people were torn*

Slavery was not outlawed in the United States until the year 1865.

about slavery. And as new states joined the nation, they had to decide if they were going to be slave states or not. Many speeches, like the one Frederick Douglass made in New York, inspired people to think even harder.

Corinthian Hall was so named because of its large Corinthian-style columns.

“Please don’t spill. Please don’t spill,” Jacob Williams muttered to himself as he carefully balanced a heavy tray full of dishes. It was his final shift of the day. As he carried food from table to table, all he could think about were his friends outside, playing without him.

But he was excited to be inside the newly built Corinthian Hall. The room was the biggest he had ever seen. At least 500 people were seated on **risers** and at tables. Chandeliers hung from the ceiling. Giant columns were at the front where the speakers stood. Huge windows on both sides of the room let in the sunlight, reminding Jacob of what he was missing.

"Get moving," a voice whispered from behind him. Charles, his boss, motioned him to hurry up with his tray of dishes. "Get to the kitchen," he said. "Our next speaker is starting, and I need people to pay attention to him, not to you!"

Putting his tray down in the kitchen, Jacob was delighted that his shift was over. He tore off his apron and quietly snuck through Corinthian Hall, heading for the door. But he stopped when he heard the next speaker being introduced . . . Frederick Douglass. Jacob had heard about him. Douglass was a former slave who traveled all over the country giving speeches. He had even written a few books.

Anna Murray helped Douglass escape slavery. She married him in 1838.

“I thought we were here to celebrate the anniversary of the Declaration of Independence,” Jacob heard one woman mutter.

“Julia and her Ladies’ Anti-Slavery Society invited him,” another woman replied.

A man sitting nearby snorted. “Humph! He may be a free man, but he is still not like us.”

Jacob looked at the front of the room. An impressive black man stood at the **podium**. He wore a dark suit with a shiny satin vest under his jacket.

After Anna's death, Douglass married Helen Pitts (right) in 1884.

Harriet Tubman helped more than 300 slaves escape to freedom.

"That's him," someone whispered.

Douglass looked out over the room with a thoughtful, intelligent gaze. He cleared his throat and began speaking.

"Mr. President, friends, and fellow citizens: He who could address this audience without a **quailing** sensation has stronger nerves than I have. I do not remember ever to have appeared as a speaker before any assembly more shrinkingly, nor with greater distrust of my ability, than I do this day."

Jacob realized that Douglass was pointing out that he knew there were people in this audience who probably did not like him or want to hear the words of an educated black man. Jacob was not one of those people. Jacob couldn't understand how Mr. Douglass could question his own abilities. People came from all over the nation to hear him speak. Jacob quietly found a seat in the back and pulled his journal out of his pocket.

The Ladies' Anti-Slavery Society

In the summer of 1851, notices began popping up throughout Rochester, New York. They invited women who believed slavery was "an evil that ought not to exist" to join the newly formed anti-slavery group. One of the first to join was Julia Griffiths, who served as the group's treasurer. Over the first year, the organization grew to 19 members. They raised funds by selling handmade items and charging people to see speakers like Douglass. Over the years, the Ladies' Anti-Slavery Society held festivals, published and sold essays, and sponsored a lecture series. The money they raised was used to help fund anti-slavery newspapers and literature. It also helped escaped slaves get across the border to Canada and freedom.

CHAPTER 2

Rejoice or Mourn?

For the first few minutes of his speech, Frederick Douglass praised the people behind the nation's Declaration of Independence. "Fellow citizens, I am not wanting in respect for the fathers of this republic. The signers of the Declaration of Independence were brave men," he stated. "They were statesmen, patriots and heroes, and for the good they did, and the principles they contended for, I will unite with you to honor their memory."

Looking around the room, Jacob could see people nodding and smiling in agreement with his words. But then, Douglass's voice changed. "Fellow citizens, pardon me, allow me to ask, why am

The Fourth of July, also called Independence Day, has been celebrated since 1777.

Douglass met with Abraham Lincoln in 1863 to discuss the recruitment of African American soldiers during the Civil War.

I called upon to speak here today?" he said. "What have I, or those I represent, to do with your national independence?" Jacob watched as people's foreheads wrinkled, their heads tipped. A low murmur ran through the room. Then Douglass said, "This Fourth of July is yours, not mine. You may rejoice, I must mourn."

Voices rose quickly throughout the hall. What was Douglass saying? Jacob wondered, scribbling the speaker's words directly into his journal. For the next few minutes, he listened as Douglass explained how even though this was a day meant to honor independence and freedom, slaves experienced neither.

"What, to the American slave, is your Fourth of July?" Douglass asked passionately. "I answer: a day that reveals to him, more than all other days in the year, the gross injustice and cruelty to which he is the constant victim."

If people there recognized that African Americans are humans and that freedom is a right, why then, he asked, was slavery still allowed to exist? As he spoke, he got louder and louder, asking people to work harder and do more to end slavery. "For it is not light that is needed, but fire; it is not the gentle shower, but thunder. We need the storm, the whirlwind, and the earthquake," he stated.

Frederick Douglass was the most photographed individual of the 19th century.

Although the room was mainly full of abolitionists, they were still startled to hear Douglass say that the work they were doing simply was not enough.

"What does the man expect us to do?" Jacob heard someone say.

"He's right," another voice whispered. "We must fight harder."

It was clear a few people in the audience disliked Douglass's speech so far, Jacob thought. But many more people were inspired by his words.

The Life of Frederick Douglass

Frederick Augustus Washington Bailey (Douglass) was born in 1818 in Maryland. He learned how to read and write at an early age. For years, he was a slave, and he was often mistreated and beaten by his owners. At age 20, he disguised himself as a free sailor and escaped to freedom in the North, changing his name so he could not be tracked down. During his lifetime, Douglass was a popular speaker and author. He even served as a **consultant** *to four different presidents. He died in 1895.*

CHAPTER 3

Nations Linked

As he sat in Corinthian Hall, Jacob wrote as quickly as he could. He didn't want to miss any of the important ideas that Frederick Douglass was sharing with the crowd. The room was silent, except for the occasional gasp or whispered comment in the audience. Douglass painted a dark picture of the country, calling it a place of "revolting **barbarity** and shameless **hypocrisy**." Despite this, he ended his speech on a more positive note.

It was illegal for slaves to learn to read and write in many Southern states. They had to learn in secret.

"Intelligence is penetrating the darkest corners of the globe," he stated. "It makes its pathway over and under the sea, as well as on the earth. Oceans no longer divide, but link nations together. Thoughts expressed on one side of the Atlantic are distinctly heard on the other."

Abraham Lincoln issued the Emancipation Proclamation in 1863.

Jacob paused a moment to think about what Douglass had just said. Nations linked together—it was an idea he could barely comprehend. He had never even been out of New York, let alone all the way to another state or country!

After Douglass finished his speech, Jacob closed his journal and went outside. Douglass had been clear. Abolitionists were doing good work, but it was far from enough. The Fourth of July was a holiday centered on honoring freedom and independence, but many African Americans were still in chains. When would that change?

It was a question that Jacob would revisit often over the years.

A Proclamation

Many people believe that President Abraham Lincoln's **Emancipation** *Proclamation is what gave slaves their freedom. But that is only part of a longer story. The proclamation stated that "all persons held as slaves . . . are, and henceforward shall be free." There were definite limits, however. For example, this new law was only enforced in certain states. In addition, it was dependent on the North winning the Civil War. Slavery officially ended when the 13th Amendment was passed in 1865.*

CHAPTER 4

More Work to Do

The college classroom had almost no empty seats. Professor Oliver Williams's Black History class was one of the most popular on campus. He had an incredible way of bringing history to life. Instead of simply listing dates and names and locations, he told stories of what life was actually like during some of the country's most important moments in the Civil War.

"Let's pick up where we left off yesterday," Professor Williams began. He glanced around the room to make sure he had everyone's attention. "We've been learning about what it was like to be a slave

Frederick Douglass's words continue to inspire today.

in the United States. And we're learning how the writings that have emerged from that time help us better understand the division in the nation over the idea of slavery. Now let's talk about one of the most famous men in history, Frederick Douglass, from the **perspective** of someone who was lucky enough to see him in person."

Douglass's home opened in 1972, after a restoration by the National Park Service.

Reaching over to the podium, the professor picked up an old, weathered journal. "This is the journal of my great-great-great-great-great-grandfather," he said. "It has been handed down for more than six generations." He paused.

"On July 5, Douglass was asked to give a speech to help celebrate the country's independence and freedom," Professor Williams explained. "He was invited to speak at Corinthian Hall in New York by the local women abolitionists. He surprised the crowd by first praising the country and then condemning it. My ancestor, Jacob

In the first 4 months of its publication, *Narrative of the Life of Frederick Douglass, an American Slave* sold 5,000 copies.

A century after the Emancipation Proclamation, African Americans marched on Washington, DC, to demand an end to racial bias.

Williams, was actually in the audience at the time and wrote about it in this very journal. He stated, 'Douglass stands there and, with his eloquent bearing and educated vocabulary, puts to shame any notion of the black man as inferior.'"

For the next hour, Professor Williams described Douglass's famous speech from the perspective of a young boy in the crowd. After he finished, one student raised her hand. "What do you think Douglass would think of the progress we have made—or not made—since his time?" she asked.

"I'm not sure," admitted the professor. "I think he would be pleased with the progress we have made in some areas, like electing our first African American president, Barack Obama, in 2008. On the other hand, I suspect he would be angered by the racial inequality that exists in America even today. He would likely say that we still have a lot of work to do."

Professor Williams suspected that Jacob, his ancestor, would have agreed.

Another Movement

During the 1950s and 1960s, the civil rights movement swept the nation as African Americans fought for equality. While the Civil War had ended slavery, a century later, African Americans continued to face violence, **discrimination**, *and injustice. Leaders of the civil rights movement were inspired by Douglass's words and gave them renewed meaning. Figures like Rosa Parks and Martin Luther King Jr. organized events like the Montgomery Bus Boycott and the March on Washington. Ultimately, these efforts would lead to the signing of the Civil Rights Act of 1964. However, the fight of racial equality is not over and continues even today.*

TIMELINE

1847

Douglass establishes an abolitionist newspaper, *The North Star*.

1841

Douglass speaks at the Massachusetts Anti-Slavery Society convention.

1830

1840

1838

Frederick Douglass escapes slavery.

1845

Douglass publishes *Narrative of the Life of Frederick Douglass, an American Slave*.

1850

1852

Douglass gives his famous Fourth of July speech in Rochester on July 5.

1860

1863

The Emancipation Proclamation is issued.

1850

The Fugitive Slave Act is passed.

1861

The Civil War begins.

1865

The Civil War ends.

Speech Highlight

"What, to the American slave, is your Fourth of July? I answer: a day that reveals to him, more than all other days in the year, the gross injustice and cruelty to which he is the constant victim. To him, your celebration is a sham; your boasted liberty, an unholy license; your national greatness, swelling vanity; your sounds of rejoicing are empty and heartless; your denunciations of tyrants, brass fronted impudence; your shouts of liberty and equality, hollow mockery; your prayers and hymns, your sermons and thanksgivings, with all your religious parade, and solemnity, are, to him, mere bombast, fraud, deception, impiety, and hypocrisy—a thin veil to cover up crimes which would disgrace a nation of savages."

Read the full speech at https://teachingamericanhistory.org/library/document/what-to-the-slave-is-the-fourth-of-july.

Research and Act

Frederick Douglass shared his ideas through writings and speeches. In his Fourth of July speech, he pointed out that the country had much to be proud of but also much to learn.

Research

Do some reading about a civil rights issue you see happening today. Research ways to help.

Act

Imagine Frederick Douglass was going to make a speech about the issue you've been researching. Write a title for his speech and outline three to five main points you think he would include.

Further Reading

Bolden, Tonya. *Facing Frederick: The Life of Frederick Douglass, a Monumental American Man.* New York, NY: Abrams Books for Young Readers, 2017.

Freedman, Russell. *Abraham Lincoln and Frederick Douglass: The Story Behind an American Friendship.* Boston, MA: Houghton Mifflin Harcourt, 2016.

Prince, April Jones. *Who Was Frederick Douglass?* New York, NY: Grosset and Dunlap, 2014.

Slade, Suzanne. *Friends for Freedom: The Story of Susan B. Anthony and Frederick Douglass.* Watertown, MA: Charlesbridge, 2014.

GLOSSARY

abolitionists (ab-uh-LISH-uh-nists) people who worked to put an end to slavery

barbarity (bar-BEHR-uh-tee) cruelty

consultant (kuhn-SUHL-tuhnt) an expert in a particular field who is hired by others to give advice

discrimination (dis-krim-ih-NAY-shuhn) unfair behavior toward others based on differences in things such as race, age, or gender

emancipation (ih-man-suh-PAY-shuhn) freedom

hypocrisy (hih-PAH-krih-see) claiming or pretending to have certain beliefs that are actually the opposite of what one believes

perspective (pur-SPEK-tiv) a particular way of looking at something

podium (POH-dee-uhm) a stand with a surface for holding papers, for use by a person giving a speech

quailing (KWAYL-ing) feeling fear

risers (RIZE-urz) groups of movable steps on which people sit or stand to see or be seen better

INDEX